OUTLAWED by Grace

MYCHAILO KAZYBRID.

Bible-based resources for youth groups

Ten sessions on Galatians for 13-18 year olds

Written by Ian Kitchen & Steve Tilley

Edited by Mark Tomlinson

OUTLAWED BY GRACE

How to use this book
NOTES FOR YOUTH LEADERS

This is a difficult page to write. How far back do you start? Should we begin with, 'First, learn to read', or 'First, get a bunch of young people together'. No, that would be insulting, so we've made a few assumptions.

1. We've assumed that you are doing church-based, Christian youth work with teenagers aged 12-20.

2. We've assumed you want to use the Bible with this group.

3. We've assumed that you've done this before, because Galatians is a tough book and we wouldn't advise starting with it.

If the first two assumptions are wrong you may need to do a few other things before this book is really useful. If the third assumption is wrong then keep 'Outlawed By Grace' for a while and start your group off with something simpler. CPAS and Covenanters can both advise you on this.

*   We've not assumed that your group is very big.

*   We've not assumed that your group are all book worms, although there are some special activities and opportunities for those who are.

*   We've not assumed that you are a professional, full-time, or a Christian youth minister, though you can still use the book if you are.

We believe that a small group with less than average reading skills can still get a lot out of a difficult Bible book.

'Outlawed By Grace' has been written in ten individual sessions to help you work through Galatians with your group. Please don't do all ten in a row. Galatians is a difficult book and we recommend doing two or three sessions and then taking a break. Other books from CPAS and Covenanters, such as 'Pressure Points' or 'Just About Coping' give you sessions you can use as 'one-offs' to break up your programme.

Each session of 'Outlawed By Grace' is divided into:
◆ **Teaching Point**
◆ **Group Aim**
✎ **Equipment Checklist**
☞ **Leaders' Guide**
☞ **Bible Background**
➤ **Starting It, Teaching It and Doing It – The main teaching content,**
✍ **Work-out – copyright-free, photocopyable pages for members.**

HOW TO USE THIS BOOK

Preparation Pray through the content and for the members of your group.

Prepare well in advance. Some of the sessions have preparation that needs to be started well in advance. Be in the habit of reading things through three or four weeks ahead. That way you will get a feel for the material, be able to start your preparation and will probably come up with better ideas than we have.

Read the passage, and any appropriate commentaries, thoroughly.

Select the material you are going to use. We have used a code throughout this book:

 **Essential** – Strongly recommended for inclusion and should provide a core session of about thirty minutes.

 Desirable – Good supplementary material to take your session up to about an hour in length.

 Additional – Extra material for longer meetings or to provide variety for groups of different age or ability.

Relationships We say this in all our books so there is a danger of it getting boring, but, boring or not, here goes; **relationships are important**. People are more important than programmes. You need to be in a relationship with your young people. If you meet for an hour, once a week it will be six months before you have spent a day with them.

Share your life with them and they will learn about the Christian life from being with you. If your life and teaching is consistent they will want to know more. If there is inconsistency, praise God that the teenagers have helped you identify it, then sort your life out. Sorry if that sounded rather abrupt.

Finally We've enjoyed preparing this material. CYFA and Covenanters try to produce two new books like this every year. We love feedback. Tell us what worked and what didn't. Tell us anything that will help us to write more useful material in the future. We are always on the look out for groups to trial our material. If you are interested in using draft sessions at the pre-design stage then why not ask if you can help us to help others.

Happy Teaching.

➤ GALATIANS: AN OVERVIEW

False teachers. They really are a nuisance. Trouble is, normally only true teachers are equipped to spot the false ones. Which brings us, rather cleverly if you don't mind us saying so, on to Galatians.

HOW TO USE THIS BOOK

Paul, true teacher, Apostle and church planter to the Gentile (non-Jewish) world, had visited the Roman province of Galatia about thirteen years after Jesus' resurrection. The visit is described in **Acts Chapters 13 & 14**. He converted people from both Jewish and Gentile backgrounds. He preached that God's gift of new, and eternal, life came through faith in Jesus. No problem so far. What happened next?

Paul left and enter the baddies; we don't know precisely who they were. Their message appears to have been that to be a Christian you had to become a Jew first, then have faith in Jesus. It followed from this that Gentile converts had to be brought up to scratch with all the rituals and ceremonies of Judaism; and blokes had to be circumcised.

Galatians is Paul's corrective to this dodgy teaching (so put that knife down). There are three clear points to his letter:

AUTHORITY The Judaizers have only the authority of tradition. Paul obtained his authority to preach the Gospel from Christ Himself. The Gospel supersedes the Law. Paul is astonished (**1:6**) that his readers should desert his Gospel in favour of one that came from a lesser authority. Much of **Galatians Chapters 1 & 2** is devoted to a sturdy defence of Paul's authority.

GOSPEL If the Law still had saving power, then in effect Christ died for nothing (**2:21**). Paul's ministry was to explain that the punishment due to humans for failing to keep the Law fell onto Christ on the cross (**3:1,2**). It would be stupid, argues Paul in **Galatians 3**, to exchange the power of the Holy Spirit for weak, human willpower (**3:3**). In a lengthy, allegorical piece in **Galatians 4**, Paul compares the choice facing Christians today as a choice between Abraham's sons, Ishmael and Isaac, one the son of a slave woman, the other the son of a free woman. The Galatians needed to learn to value freedom (**5:1**).

BEHAVIOUR Responding to the true Gospel, Paul argued, needed to affect all of life. Life in the Spirit was not freedom from the Law unless it was freedom to do good (**5:13**). In the final part of **Galatians** we have the passages which are probably best known; the 'acts of the sinful nature' (**5:19-21**) compared to the 'fruit of the Spirit' (**5:22 & 23**). In farming terms (no, we don't know why Paul suddenly started reading 'Farming Today') it is a matter of sowing in the field of the Spirit (**6:8**).

In his commentary, John Stott summarises his own summary thus; '...we have Christ through His Apostles to teach us, Christ through His cross to save us and Christ through His Spirit to sanctify us.'

Absolutely. Thank you.

Worship and your youth group

Worship is about giving back to God what He is worth. Clearly impossible. It is also about the whole of our lives, our service, not just the 'praisey things' we do. More than one New Testament Greek word is translated 'worship'. A word study would be well worth while.

But your youth group might want to do 'praisey' things from time to time, yet find it difficult because:
- Nobody can play an instrument
- Their voices are breaking and they're embarrassed
- There's only three of them

If these things are not a problem then you don't need us to give you a selection of songs from which to pick. Your members will have their favourites from church, or perhaps from ventures, camps and houseparties. Every year a new Spring Harvest song book comes out, featuring the latest worship songs plus many older ones that have stood the test of time.

If these things don't suit you, then how about:

- Buying 'Rave On' or 'DIY Worship' from CPAS. They'll give you loads of ideas.

- Thinking about doing something other than singing; try silence, meditation, spoken words of praise or listening to one of the many tapes or CDs that are around.

- Inviting the young people to consider their response to God and to create their own worship. This is how much of today's alternative worship scene developed.

It is good to help the young people to focus on God, particularly in the response part of each of these sessions, which we have called, 'Doing It'. Helping young people to respond to God is the essence of what you are doing in these teaching sessions. Don't limit their response to things you think they might like to do. Let their imaginations have free reign. Let them speak out.

'I am full of words, and the spirit within me compels me; inside I am like bottled-up wine, like new wineskins ready to burst. I must speak and find relief; I must open my lips and reply. I will show partiality to no-one, nor will I flatter any man; for if I were skilled in flattery, my Maker would soon take me away.' (Job's young friend Elihu almost bursts with frustration as he waits for the adults to finish, before speaking – **Job 32:18-22**).

Ice Breakers

A selection of icebreakers you might scatter through the sessions in this book. Some of them pick up the themes we'll meet in Galatians, others are sheer self-indulgence.

Colour Coded
Sit in paint chart order, so colours of tops blend into each other.

Untangle
This is an old one that's worth keeping alive. The group stands in a circle (more than one, if the group is more than a dozen people). Face inwards. Everyone reaches into the middle of the circle with their left hands and takes someone else's hand at random. Repeat the process with right hands. Then, without letting go at all, they try to untangle the resulting mess so that everyone is standing in a reshuffled circle, holding the hands of the people either side of them. It doesn't always work, particularly if you're pushed for time, but very often it does. It's always fun.

Butterfly Emerging
Tie a volunteer's hands together and insert the volunteer into an old sleeping bag (head at the open end!). Time them to see how long it takes them to escape. Allow as many people to do it as you want, but be sensitive to claustrophobia. If it seems too easy, tie a piece of rope loosely around the bag, above the volunteer's elbows.

Hangman's Circle
An individual leaves the room while the rest of the group choose a word. The individual then comes back and the group stands around him or her in a circle (judge the size of the circle according to the length of the word). The individual then has to guess the word, a letter at a time, along the lines of the old game of 'Hangman'. For every wrong letter, the group closes in a little. If the individual guesses the word, they go free. Otherwise, quite a tense atmosphere can build up. Know your group before choosing to use this activity or it can cause, rather than break, ice.

Accented Text
Choose a short Bible passage (perhaps, but not necessarily, the one you're about to study) and ask people to read it while putting on different regional accents. They can ham it up as much as they want. Progress to national accents if your group can do this without sinking into abject racism. Extrovert groups will love it.

Apple Scramble
This is one against the clock. Cut an apple into lots of thin slices and jumble them up. Then a volunteer has to rebuild the apple. Use apples of a similar size and allow as many volunteers to take part as you and your greengrocer can cope with.

Centre Point

Ask everyone to think of three characteristics they think are part of their personality. One should be more important than the others. Each person shares their three and the rest of the group note down what they think the central characteristic is. Go round the whole group and then compare people's views of each other.

Fruit Spotting

Get a lot of different fruit-flavoured sweets. Blindfold group members, give them a selection of sweets and get them to identify the flavours—you'll need to make sure you know which is which.

Complete Lemons

Ask everyone in the group to say what kind of fruit they would be, if they were a fruit. Explaining why is optional, but can be very funny.

Bit By Bit

Cut some photos of well known people's faces out of magazines. Cut them up in circles, like the rings on a target. Start with the nose and add successive rings until someone can identify the person.

Last Phone Call

If Paul wanted to get an important message to the Galatians today, he'd probably phone them. Ask the group whom they would phone if they were allowed one last phone call before the end of the world. Phoning other members of the group is not allowed.

The One and Only
Galations 1:1-17

◆ **TEACHING POINT**

God has told us what we must do to be saved from our sins.
We must guard against changing that message in any way.

◆ **GROUP AIM**

For the group to understand the importance of the Gospel and its
content, and to appreciate God's great love in revealing it to us.

✎ **EQUIPMENT CHECKLIST**
- ❏ Bibles
- ❏ *Work-Out* sheets
- ❏ Cards with elements of the Gospel
- ❏ Pencils and paper
- ❏ Darts, quoits (or similar) and target
- ❏ Evangelistic booklets
- ❏ Prizes

☞ **LEADERS' GUIDE**

Two key terms in Galatians, especially in the opening chapters, are 'Gospel' and 'apostle'. 'Gospel' means 'good news'; it is the joyful news about Jesus, not purely academic knowledge. To change the Gospel is therefore to miss the good news and to dishonour God, who planned it. No wonder Paul defends it so vigorously! An 'apostle' was a messenger with a special status, whose authority came from someone higher than himself. Paul is concerned that the Galatians should understand that this is the position he is in; he is not peddling a message that he has concocted himself. God Himself is the one who has sent this message.

It is helpful to keep the burning importance of these two ideas in mind in looking at Galatians, as Paul keeps returning to them. Let's be sure that we understand the wonder of what God has done as we try to help our group members grasp that wonder for themselves.

☞ **BIBLE BACKGROUND**

For all the sessions in this book, make time beforehand to look into the passages indicated in *Bible Background* so that you can tell the stories well and briefly to your group. This is a more helpful way of giving them the background than asking them to hop around the Bible picking up scattered pieces of information.

The story of Paul's conversion (at a time when he was called Saul) can be found in **Acts 9:1-22**. From that time on he had been preaching that only through faith in Jesus could people be saved. Others, however, were saying that obedience to the Jewish ritual laws was required in addition to faith. These people are known as 'Judaizers'. For an account of the crucial discussion among the apostles on this point see **Acts 15:1-21**. As we shall see in future sessions, the key requirement of the law on which the Judaizers focused was circumcision (see also **Acts 15:1&5**).

➤ STARTING IT

One Way

Distribute copies of the *Work-Out* sheet and challenge the group to solve the maze as quickly as they can. Offer a prize for the winner and perhaps the runners-up, but don't let it go on too long. Make the point that saying there's only one way to do something isn't necessarily intolerant, though it's often treated that way. It may just be the truth. The maker of the maze created only one way of solving it, and we're going to see that God has done the same with the number of ways we can be saved.

Bare Essentials

Galatians 1:1-5 contains the basis of the Gospel which Paul goes on to defend. Have different elements of the Gospel message, taken from these verses, stuck up on cards in random order around the room:
Lord, Jesus, gave Himself, raised from the dead, our sins, rescue, God's choice, glory

Add a few false ones:
doing good, not smoking, speaking in tongues, helping at home, etc

Ask the group, working in pairs, to pick the five words or phrases they think are the most crucial ingredients of the Christian message. Now read **verses 1-5** and check with the group what ingredients Paul thought were essential. Make the point that people will always try to introduce other things in addition, and that is what the whole letter is fighting against. Allow time for any questions members have about these verses.

➤ TEACHING IT

What A Let Down

Paul feels really let down by the Galatians, and expresses this in **verse 6**. Get the group to share examples of people letting others down; these may be from their own lives, from TV soaps or anywhere else. Use these examples to make the point that this letter is about real people, their emotions, hopes and fears. Paul is not some stern robot, coldly trying to enforce one way of thinking: he loves Jesus and the Galatians and is thrilled with gratitude for what God has done — and he doesn't want the Galatians to miss out on it.

Consequences

Give out pencils and paper and play a brisk game of consequences: sit in a circle and each member writes the name of a famous male person or fictional character on their paper. Then they fold the paper over to conceal the name and pass it on. On the paper they receive they write a female name, then fold and pass it on. Then they write a place, then what the male character said, then what the female character said, then what the outcome was. Each time they write an item, they fold the paper over and pass it on. After all these stages the papers are unfolded and the contents read out within the framework:

'(male) met (female) in (place). He said...She said...and the consequence was...'

The results of this game are usually very funny, particularly as group members are liable to introduce all sorts of in-jokes. Fortunately, none of the consequences stated in the game is likely to happen. Make the point, though, that whether or not we have the true Gospel, it has enormous consequences. If it's not right then it's *'really no Gospel at all'* (**verse 7**) and so, clearly, God won't work through it to save us.

Just Deserts

Ask the group to look at the 'crimes' listed on the *Work-Out* sheet. In pairs or threes they should suggest punishments that fit each crime. Have a small award for the most appropriate ones.

Just as false Gospels have consequences for those who believe them, they have implications too for those who peddle them. If, as we should be, we are telling others the Gospel, there's a warning to us in **verses 8 & 9**. The solution is not to avoid telling others about Jesus, in case we get it wrong, but to make sure we get it right. Studying this letter will be a massive help in doing that.

On Target

How, then, do we know that Paul's Gospel is trustworthy? **Verses 10-12** hold the key. First, Paul's only concern is to please God. Use a set of darts, quoits, or something similar to give the group an experience of aiming at a target. Explain that all Paul's thoughts and intentions are centred on God and glorifying God. He is not trying to add anything of his own to the Gospel.

Start From Here

Not only is God the focus of the Gospel, He is also its source. Paul goes on to explain this in the next part of the letter, which we will look at in Session 2. For now, read **verses 11 & 12** with the group. If they don't know the story of Paul's conversion, briefly run through it with them (see **Acts 9:1-22**).

➤ DOING IT

Go With The Gospel

It is vital that our group members know a Gospel outline to use as their basis for telling others about Jesus. Split them into pairs and give them each thirty seconds to tell their partner the Gospel. Then give pairs the chance to check what they have said against either **Galatians 1:1-5** or an outline from *'Journey into Life'*, *'Two Ways to Live'*, or a similar booklet. Encourage them to think how they might be able to introduce the Gospel into conversations in their everyday activities.

Look Ahead

Help the group to make plans for telling someone the Gospel in the coming week. It may be that they can identify one friend to whom they want to speak, or one situation where they'll be able to introduce the topic of faith. Aim that each member who is trying to follow Jesus should be able to speak of Him at some time during the week, with the confidence that comes from knowing what the Gospel is. Have a brief time of prayer about this. (If you include this activity in your session, be sure to allow time in your next meeting for feedback on how people got on.)

Summary

Summarise briefly this session, and look together at **Romans 5:1** as a memory verse – for learning either now or individually during the week. It summarises beautifully the effect of the Gospel events, and raises the subject of grace which will become more and more prominent as our study of Galatians goes on.

Pray

Have a time of prayer in small groups, focusing particularly on God's goodness in sending Jesus 'to rescue us from the present evil age'. Encourage members to pray aloud but don't force them.

MEMORY VERSE

Therefore, since we have been justified through faith, we have peace with God through our Lord Jesus Christ.

Romans 5:1

START

MAZE

FINISH

What punishments would be suitable for the following dastardly crimes?

CRIMES   PUNISHMENTS

☞ Belching in front of the Queen

☞ Eating the last chocolate biscuit

☞ Stealing your friend's boy/girlfriend

☞ Forgetting to feed the hamster

☞ Hiding your mate's CDs so he'll have
   to play yours, which he hates

☞ Cutting someone up at a road junction

Quality Controlled
Galations 1:13–2:10

◆ TEACHING POINT

Paul received the Gospel directly from God — and it was the same as that which the other apostles had received from Jesus in His earthly life.

◆ GROUP AIM

To understand how trustworthy Paul's message is and to recognise the danger of adding things to the Gospel, as these can enslave us.

✎ **EQUIPMENT CHECKLIST**

❏ Bibles
❏ *Work-Out* sheets
❏ Map of the Middle East
❏ Paper and pencils
❏ OHP/large sheet of paper

❏ Information on persecuted Christians
❏ Marshmallows, table-tennis balls, teaspoons and a bucket

☞ **LEADERS' GUIDE**

Galatians 1:13 starts 'For', so be sure to recap quickly the point made in **verses 11 & 12**; this will be a useful reinforcement of part of the previous session.

In session 1 we touched briefly on how Paul got his Gospel. Now we get some flashbacks from later in his Christian life, all centring on the fact that the Gospel he was proclaiming could be trusted as coming straight from God.

Be sure to read through session 3 well in advance: some of the preparation for it won't be possible at the last minute!

☞ **BIBLE BACKGROUND**

During the episodes that Paul refers to in **Galatians 1:13-2:10**, we hear that he and his teaching are eventually accepted by James, Peter and John – the three apostles who shared most closely in the earthly ministry of Jesus (see **Matthew 17:1ff** and **Matthew 26:36ff**). This acceptance was sealed at a Council in Jerusalem, possibly but not necessarily the one reported in **Acts chapter 15**.

For Barnabas, whom Paul took to Jerusalem with him, see **Acts 4:36-37** and **Acts 9:26-28**. Paul's other companion, Titus, is not mentioned in Acts but clearly had special concern for the churches in Corinth and Crete (see Paul's letters to the **Corinthians** and to **Titus**).

One essential piece of Bible knowledge which your group will need is the distinction between Jews and Gentiles. **Genesis 12:1-3** recounts God's initial promise to Abraham that his descendants (the Jews) would be God's special people. After this, the division between Jews and Gentiles (everybody else) was thought to be insurmountable. Paul in Galatians fiercely attacks the idea that God cannot or will not save Gentiles as well, or that they must adopt Jewish religious rules to win God's favour. If your group are not aware of this issue you need to introduce them to it in the context of **Galatians 2:3&7**, though we won't be looking at it in detail until later sessions.

➤ STARTING IT

Headliners

✪ ✪ ✪

Skim through **Galatians 1:13-22** to make the point that Paul didn't check out the message that he'd received from Christ with anyone else, so there was no way it could have been changed.

If you can show a map of the places mentioned, that will help people to grasp what Paul is saying. Then look at **verse 23**. This must have been a mind-boggling and utterly thrilling report for the Judean churches to hear!

Give the group a minute or so, working on their own, to come up with a one-line tabloid headline which sums up the way they think people see them. As an example, give them Paul's: 'Ex-persecutor preaches the faith!!' Each should put his/her headline on a sheet of paper and draw a quick self-portrait by it in place of a photograph. Put all the headlines up on an OHP or large sheet of paper or acetate, as a summary of the group.

Then look at **verse 24**. Discuss how many of the headlines would lead people to praise God. Would any of them lead in the opposite direction? If you feel it's appropriate, allow a moment for silent prayer before moving on.

Entry Tickets

✪ ✪ ✪

➤ TEACHING IT

Point out to the group that Paul must have been tempted to boast about the content of **verses 23 & 24** — but he immediately moves on to what he sees as the most important thing, which is not him but his message. As we saw in session 1, the essence of this is that people are saved through Jesus' death. Following certain rules and ceremonies is not necessary.

The particular rule which often reared its head was circumcision (make sure your group know what this is!) This was an essential sign of being part of God's people until Jesus came, but Paul was adamant that it was no longer necessary — and the rest of the church, who were mainly Jewish, were beginning to be convinced (**verses 2&3**).

Give the group copies of the *Work-Out* sheet and ask them to work in groups to identify things today which act as ways into a part of society or as signs of belonging to a particular group. (If it suits your group better, don't bother with the sheets, just ask them to think about the questions.) Then explain that these things are acting in the same way as circumcision, though the 'rules' are probably not quite so rigid. In secular society this may not matter, though some things may assume far too much importance and become unhealthy for Christians. However, in the church we must be very careful of putting up this sort of barrier which adds other requirements to the Gospel; nor must we allow other people to do so.

Allow discussion to develop from this if group members want to talk further.

Stand Up For...

Ask the group to brainstorm about things which people they know, or know of, would make a stand for even if it put them in danger. Examples might be allegiance to a football team, terrorists' allegiance to their cause, and so on. Write up the ideas on an OHP or a large sheet of paper.

Ask if the group members would make a similar stand for anything or anyone. Add these to the list if so. Then look at **verses 4 & 5**. Paul made such a stand against fierce opposition (and elsewhere we hear that his very life was often in danger — eg **Acts 14:19**) for the sake of the Gospel.

See if anyone knows of areas of the world where Christians are in danger now because of the Gospel. Be prepared with information from a resource like Operation World (published by STL Publications) in case you need to supply it. Have a short time of prayer for such people, and of thanks that people have stood up in the past for the true Gospel so that it has survived many onslaughts over the centuries.

Going Equipped

➤ DOING IT

Divide the group into 2 or more teams (adjust the following activities appropriately if you need to use more than 2 teams). Give one team a marshmallow and the other a table-tennis ball, and give each individual a teaspoon.

Activity 1 is an 'egg and spoon race' using these items.

Activity 2 is to bounce the ball/mallow off a wall into a bucket 2 feet or more away from the wall.

Activity 3 is a game of hockey (warn the teams about clashing heads), using first the mallow and then the table-tennis ball. You'll need plenty of spares of each!

Have a quick debrief, focusing on which activity or activities were best suited to the team with the ball and which to the team with the marshmallow. It's all a question of what you're equipped with.

God had particularly equipped Paul to work among one set of people, and had equipped Peter to work among others (**verses 7 & 8**). So what happened next? They went and got on with the work (**verse 9**)! Ask the group to think about and share ideas on where they might put their abilities and concerns to work for the Gospel, now and later on in life.

Summary

Summarise briefly this session, and look together at **Galatians 2:5** as a memory verse — for learning either now or individually during the week. It should be a useful reminder of how important the Gospel is, and how dangerous it is to add extra requirements to it.

Pray

Have a time for prayer, either aloud or in silence, focusing particularly on the importance of the Gospel, God's goodness in preserving it through the centuries, and our part in passing it on accurately today.

MEMORY VERSE

We did not give in to them for a moment, so that the truth of the Gospel might remain with you.

Galatians 2:5

What things act as ways of entry into, or signs of belonging to, the following groups of people?

* Ravers

* The Police

* Jungle music followers

* Trainspotters

* Trekkies

* Classical musicians

* My group of mates

* Actors

* Football fans

* My local church

Don't Spit On The Cross

Galatians 2:11-21

◆ TEACHING POINT

God's grace and Christ's death are our foundation as Christians. We work with God so that our lives match up to our belief.

◆ GROUP AIM

To understand the centrality of the crucifixion and the freedom it gives us, with Christ living in us to change us.

✎ **EQUIPMENT CHECKLIST**

❑ Bibles
❑ Vox Pop tape or video
❑ *Work-Out* sheets

❑ Adverts from newspapers and magazines
❑ Cross, another object, wire hoops

☞ **LEADERS' GUIDE**

It will be helpful to collect some 'Vox Pop' comments on a tape or video for use in this session. Either do it yourself or, better, involve the group. Ask people in your area, 'What do you think is the one main idea of the Christian faith – what's it all about?' If their answer is along the lines of 'Going to heaven' ask, 'How?'

One of the best ways to do this is at a local secondary school but ensure you have permission from the school and do the recording during a lunch-hour or as they leave after school. It is important to get views from non-Christian/non church people.

In this session, **verses 17-21** are difficult to grasp but are absolutely key; challenge your group, if need be, to make the effort to understand them.

☞ **BIBLE BACKGROUND**

Verses 15 & 16 hold the key to understanding the issue underlying **verses 11-14**. Then **verse 17** holds a kind of unspoken question from Paul's opponents: 'You're relying on Christ but you still sin – is that OK by Jesus?' The answer is 'no', and **verses 18-21** explain why, nonetheless, we focus on what Jesus has done and not on what we do.

The other side of the coin, how we ought to live given that Jesus has died for us, is dealt with in the second half of **chapter 5** and **chapter 6** (sessions 9 and 10 of this resource).

➤ STARTING IT

Advert Challenge

Cut a load of adverts out of newspapers and magazines and have them face down in a pile. Everyone takes one at random, not showing anyone else what it is. Then have people working in pairs telling each other what the product is and six things about it mentioned in their advertisement — but the six things must include one or more pieces of information about it which they have made up. The other member of the pair is allowed to challenge at any stage when they think they're being told false information. A turn finishes after one correct or two incorrect challenges, or if the player describing the advert states all six bits of information without a correct challenge.

You might play several rounds of this if you have enough advertisements or play it as a knock-out tournament. Have some brief feedback on the best pieces of false information which people managed to get past their partners, and on how people felt about having to challenge what they were being told.

Speak Up

In the whole group, ask members to chip in examples of times when they've wanted to speak up against someone or something and;
> a) didn't because they were afraid, and
> b) did.

Mention some wrong things they'll know about from the local or national news and see if they think they would speak up against them.

➤ TEACHING IT

What's The Problem?

Give some brief input about why it was so important for Paul to speak up here: it was not just that Peter was wrong, but what he was wrong about (**verse 16**). His shifting back to acceptance of the Jew/Gentile distinction and the requirements of the Law attacked the basis of the Christian faith. In effect he was trying to 'rebuild what was destroyed' (see **verse 18**) and it was a harmful diversion from the true way of being right with God..

What Do We Have To Do?

Back in the first half of **chapter 1** we saw how Paul stressed the overwhelming importance of the Gospel. We also looked at the ingredients of the Gospel message. Now in **verse 16** we find stated the key to sharing in the salvation of which the Gospel speaks.

As the repetition within **verse 16** makes clear, there is a huge divide between observing the Law and faith in Christ. Introduce the 'Vox Pop' material you or the group have gathered previously. Listen to it together and see which side of the divide most people come down on in their view of the basic ingredient of Christianity.

Unless you've made a point of asking well taught, evangelical Christians the chances are that most people's views will be on the 'observing the Law' side, even if they're couched in terms of 'love' or 'being nice to people'! Discuss with the group the views they've seen or heard. Do these fit in with what their friends would think? There's a challenge here for many of us in being able to explain **why** faith in Jesus is the right way.

Work-Out

Read through **verses 17-21** and use the *Work-Out* sheet to help people understand these verses. You may be able to get people beforehand to prepare a sketch based on the presentation on the *Work-Out* sheet: this may help members to remember the essential points. Give plenty of opportunity for people to check their understanding of the verses.

In The Middle

Put in the middle of the floor a small cross and some other object, marked 'Law', 'DIY' or something similar. Provide the group with some hoops (which can be quickly made out of stiff wire) which will go over the cross but not quite over the other object. Have a game of throwing the hoops over the objects. Don't let on that half the game is impossible, and perhaps award more points for ringing the other object to encourage people to try for that one. Eventually own up.

Point out how the cross is central to salvation and that, although we often want to go down the route of gaining salvation for ourselves, that's plain impossible. **Verse 21** makes it clear that if we try that route we're saying that Jesus death was a complete waste of time; in effect we're spitting on the cross and saying it's worthless.

Real Life

The great thing is that trusting in the work of the cross gives us real life. Look together at **verse 20**. If we won't rely on Jesus' death and resurrection then we can't gain what **verse 20** is talking about, but if we accept Jesus' work on the cross this life is ours – and it's Jesus' wonderful, risen life. Ask the group for examples of times when triumph has come out of apparent or near disaster. That's exactly what has happened through the cross because Jesus loved us and gave Himself for us, and we can share in the triumph and all the great things that flow from it.

➤ DOING IT

They're Watching!

Verse 17 and the beginning of **verse 14** are useful reminders to us that, although salvation comes through what Jesus has done, people around us will still notice when we sin and will find this an obstacle to taking our message seriously.

Ask group members to think of things which they do or avoid doing which might lead people to question them in this way. Then they should mark (individually and in confidence!) these things on the target on the *Work-Out* sheet, according to how serious they think they are: major things in the bulls-eye, smaller things further out.

Remind them that all sin comes under the question and answer implied in **verse 17**: 'Does Jesus like it?' 'No!' It may be useful to spend a couple of minutes in quiet prayer now.

Summary

Summarise briefly this session, and look together at **Galatians 2:20** as a memory verse — for learning either now or individually during the week. It's a tremendous reminder of how the central point of Christianity is the cross and of the astonishing nature of the new life God gives to those who trust Him.

Pray

Have a time of thanksgiving for what God has done, and encourage the group to plan to thank God daily in the next week for Jesus' crucifixion and resurrection and the life that comes to us through them.

MEMORY VERSE

I have been crucified with Christ and I no longer live, but Christ lives in me. The life I live in the body, I live by faith in the Son of God, who loved me and gave himself for me.

Galatians 2:20

WORK-OUT

Presentation: verses 17-21

➤ Yes, we still do things which offend God
But for a solution – don't go back to the law, trying to make yourself perfect!

➤ Life comes through Jesus.
The same process breaks the hold on us of sin. So the law (which highlights our sin) loses its hold too.

➤ If we try to rely on ourselves we're refusing all benefit from what Jesus has done.

TARGET

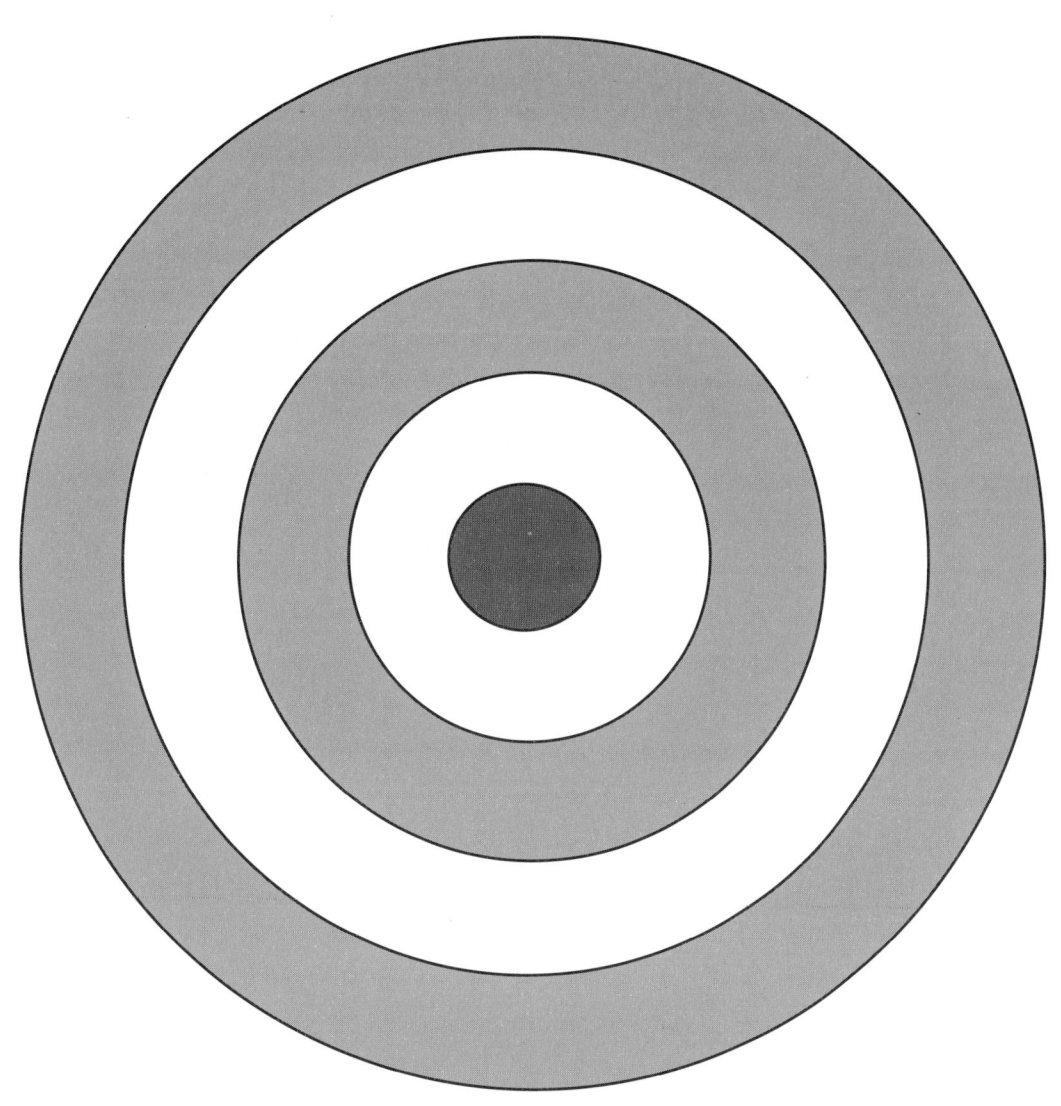

Faith, No Less
Galatians 3:1-14

◆ TEACHING POINT
That the Gospel is nothing more, and nothing less, than Jesus Christ crucified.

◆ GROUP AIM
That the group, and any guests, should understand that the only requirement of the Gospel is the faith of the believer.

✎ **EQUIPMENT CHECKLIST**

- ❑ Bibles or copies of the passage
- ❑ Copies of the cards from the *Work-Out* sheet
- ❑ A glove and a carrot
- ❑ Wood, nails or other equipment to make a cross

☞ **LEADERS' GUIDE**

Some people get very uptight about how well they are serving God. Others seem so laid back about service, they just enjoy being Christians. The Christian life is a balancing act. The Gospel is about what God has done for us. Service is the response of the faithful follower.

In this session we will be, unashamedly, ignoring all references to service and helping you to make sure your members have heard and understood the Gospel. It would be a good session in which to have evangelistic booklets handy. *'Journey Into Life'* has stood the test of time, as has *'Two Ways To Live'*, but there are other ones you may prefer for local use.

It would also be a good session to invite newcomers to, especially since the group have recently done the work on understanding and explaining the Gospel from Session 1.

☞ **BIBLE BACKGROUND**

Paul has spent much of the first two chapters of Galatians defending himself. Now he turns to a clear defence of the Gospel.

We have established that some people were suggesting that to be a Christian you first had to become a Jew. This would have involved Gentile converts in struggling to keep the Old Testament laws, observing festivals, obeying restrictive eating habits and the men being circumcised.

Paul's letter explains why these 'Judaizers' were wrong. (See *Bible Background* to Session 1 for an explanation of this term.) In this section he suggests, quite strongly, that the Galatians have been very foolish to allow themselves to be hoodwinked.

Although there are some very clever people around, and always have been, trying to add bits to God's word here and there (Mormons, Christian Scientists etc), it is up to us not to be fooled.

Paul uses a three-pronged argument to persuade the Galatians that they have been wrong. Firstly he asks them to examine their own experience (**verses 2-5**). They received the Holy Spirit not by anything they did, but by believing the Gospel they heard, as set out by Paul.

Secondly, Paul points to the faith of Abraham (**verses 6-9**). If the Judaizers have been focusing on the Law then their Old Testament hero must be Moses. Paul goes back earlier than Moses to give his argument credibility. Abraham was reckoned righteous because of his faith, not because of his works. (However as background reading, be aware of James' words in **James 2:20-24**. There is a place for works as well and Abraham is again used as the focus of the argument).

Thirdly, Paul compares the folly of trying to reach God by keeping the Law with allowing God to reach you by virtue of faith alone (**verses 8-14**). There is no comparison. Discipleship begins and ends at the foot of the cross. What God has done for us is of far more worth than anything we have done for Him.

➤ STARTING IT

Don't Be A Fool

Introduce this study by thinking about foolishness. Photocopy the *Work-Out* sheet 'Foolish Situations' and cut out each situation as cards. These introduce a situation. Ask members, working in pairs, to come up with a suggestion of the most foolish thing that could possibly happen next. For groups with a dramatic leaning you could ask the pairs to improvise a short sketch to demonstrate.

Wrong Again

If you can get hold of a copy of Stephen Pile's 'The Book of Heroic Failures' then a few excerpts from this will make an entertaining start.

During both of these exercises you could play some music with the word 'fool' in it. We thought of 'Won't Get Fooled Again', 'Fool On The Hill', 'Fool To Cry', 'Fool If You Think It's Over' and 'These Foolish Things'. Just shows how old we are. Bet you can do better. There's always 'Fools Gold' by the Stone Roses. (Someone younger than us told us that one).

➤ TEACHING IT

Missing Words

Read out the passage to everyone without any great enthusiasm or inflection in your voice. Tell members to keep their Bibles shut and listen. At the end, hand out photocopies of the passage from the *Work-Out* sheet with the missing words. Get members working in pairs or small groups if you want, to fill in the gaps. Read the passage again, stopping for their answers. Have a prize for the person who, in your opinion, entered into the spirit of the competition most appropriately.

Explain that the missing words, faith, law, belief and Spirit, will be the key words for the session.

Fooled You

Put on a glove, out of sight of the members. Fold your index finger into the palm of your hand and use a carrot to replace that finger.

Stand in front of everyone and slowly, and dramatically, break your own finger. (It makes a lovely snapping noise but we suggest it is less painful if you actually break the carrot). Quickly reveal the hoax before too many members pass out.

Read **verse 1**. Explain that the centrepiece of the Gospel is Jesus Christ crucified. We are all very easily fooled, but we should not be fooled into thinking that anything else is the focus of the Gospel.

Personal Experience

Use personal testimonies from members and leaders to emphasise that the Gospel is sufficient. You could either brief people the week before to come prepared to share, or take volunteers now. After each testimony draw out areas where the person realised that the Gospel was a matter of faith and response, not works.

At the end, get someone to read **Galatians 3:2-5**.

Cross Eyed

One of the really good reasons for having a cross in a church as the focal point is to remind us that we concentrate on Christ crucified. But it is an empty cross because He is remembered as alive beyond the cross. Why not make a cross for your meeting place. If it is a rough hewn thing then that will better remind you of it as an instrument of torture.

Abraham

What does the group remember about Abraham? Have a brainstorm. Be prepared to offer some ideas yourself if the group is not forthcoming. You can read his story in **Genesis chapter 12** onwards. (There is an excellent summary page in 'The Bible From Scratch' by Simon Jenkins.)

Explain that Paul's argument relies on his

hearers being familiar with Abraham and that he predates Moses. (See *Bible Background*). Paul uses Abraham as an example of a person of faith.

Two Ways To Live

You're going to have to do some serious input at some point in this session.

The fact is that both the Law and Jesus Christ appear to come from God, for the same purpose — to make us holy. You will need to explain how faith is now the only alternative since Jesus birth, death and resurrection. The moral law remains God's instruction to us, but the ceremonial law is no longer necessary.

If we go on trying to get to God through our own efforts and following instructions about behaviour we are booked for failure. Only by grace shall we be saved.

If you know the song 'Only By Grace' you could sing it at this point.

➤ DOING IT

Memory Verse

The memory verse in this session is not from the passage; not even from the same book. It is a great summary of the Gospel though. Read and learn together **1 Peter 2:24**.

The Way

Take a moment to set out the key facts of the Gospel, perhaps using visual aids, and challenge any who may not have responded to Christ before.

Pray for any who do, and talk to them afterwards for a while to make sure they understand the commitment they have made and to give them any suitable literature.

MEMORY VERSE

He himself bore our sins in his body on the tree, so that we might die to sins and live for righteousness; by his wounds you have been healed.

1 Peter 2:24

FOOLISH SITUATIONS:

☞ Someone asks you to look after a small parcel for a few days.

☞ You notice that the gravel pit at the bottom of your road is iced over.

☞ You are sitting in your living room when you smell gas.

☞ Your best friend tells you that she is upset because her dog has just died.

Missing words

You foolish Galatians! Who has bewitched you? Before your very eyes Jesus Christ was clearly portrayed as crucified. I would like to learn just one thing from you: Did you receive the ………. by observing the ………., or by ……………. what you heard. Are you so foolish? After beginning with the ……….., are you now trying to attain your goal by human effort? Have you suffered so much for nothing – if it really was for nothing? Does God give you His ………. and work miracles among you because you observe the …….., or because you ……………. what you heard?

Consider Abraham: 'He …………….. God, and it was credited to him as righteousness.' Under-tand, then, that those who …………… are children of Abraham. The Scripture foresaw that God would justify the Gentiles by ………….., and announced the Gospel in advance to Abraham: 'All nations will be blessed through you.' So those who have …………. are blessed along with Abraham, the man of ….. ……….

All who rely on observing the …….. are under a curse, for it is written: 'Cursed is everyone who does not continue to do everything written in the Book of the ……….' Clearly no-one is justified before God by the ………. because, 'The righteous will live by ……….' The ………. is not based on ……….; on the contrary; 'The man who does these things will live by them.' Christ redeemed us from the curse of the ……….. by becoming a curse for us, for it is written: 'Cursed is everyone who is hanged on a tree.' He redeemed us in order that the blessing given to Abraham might come to the Gentiles through Christ Jesus, so that by …………. we might receive the promise of the ………. .

These are the words you will need: *believe (x2)* *believed* | *believing* *faith (x6)* | *law (x6)* *Law* | *Spirit (x4)*

Captivating Freedom
Galatians 3:15-29

◆ **TEACHING POINT**
Faith is liberating.

◆ **GROUP AIM**
That the group would understand the joy of freedom in Christ.

✎ **EQUIPMENT CHECKLIST**
- ❏ Bibles
- ❏ *Work-Out* Sheets
- ❏ Pencils
- ❏ Prepared talk and visual aids

☞ **LEADERS' GUIDE**

It's really disappointing when someone makes you a nice promise and then later attaches conditions to that promise. It looks like that's what God does here, but it's not the case.

The only way you can show this clearly to your group is to work through the passage steadily and properly.

☞ **BIBLE BACKGROUND**

Verses 15-18 - A will cannot be altered. The aspirations of the deceased cannot change. God's promises remain, equally unchanged. The Law did not annul the promise of God.

Verses 19-22 - The law doesn't save us, but it does tell us that we need saving. The law sheds light on God's promise.

The Judaizers held that the law superseded the promise (check Session 4 again for more information). Paul's approach takes the whole of God's word seriously — the law confirms the promise, points us to the promise and tells us that we can't do without the promise. Paul teaches the unity of the Bible.

Perhaps we have been, in the past, too speedy to tell people the Gospel without convicting them of sin first. In emphasising the law this is the only valid point the Judaizers make.

Verses 15-22 are a review of biblical history, from Abraham (**Genesis chapter 12** onwards) to Moses (**Exodus chapter 2** onwards) to Jesus Christ. If we only have the law available from which to learn about God, it is like:
- Prison (**verse 23**)
- A strict tutor (a better translation of 'put in charge' verse **24**)

But now faith has come (**verse 25**) we are free.

This freedom is not just limited freedom. We are so free that under Christ all the old differences and rivalries between races, hierarchies and sexes are gone (**verse 28**)

➤ STARTING IT

Sting

There's a track on 'Dream Of The Blue Turtles' by Sting called '(If You Love Someone) Set Them Free.' It's not exactly about the same sort of relationship as Christ and His people, but it leads us into the same area. Play it if you can. You could play 'Free As A Bird' by The Beatles if you prefer, but we thought it was a dreadful song.

Contradictions

Many things seem contradictory. The world is a confusing place. You'll know this if you read the sort of magazine that gives you a diet on page three and a recipe for chocolate cake on page seventeen.

Talk, or brainstorm, some of the contradictory things in this life.

Introduce the idea that having rules can be liberating. Read **verses 15-22**.

➤ TEACHING IT

No Rules

What would the world be like without rules? If necessary break up into small groups and discuss what the key benefits are of having rules.

If you fancy a more specific discussion you could consider:

> 'Telling a child not to touch the cooker may seem to be a restriction to its liberty, but having bandages on its hands will be a worse restriction.'

From this you need to go on to explain why God, who promised good things to Abraham, had to give Moses the law in order to help His people accept the promise.

Elevation

Using the *Work-Out* sheet, list the sort of rules that churches can initiate to becoming a way to God, e.g. 'You need to go to a housegroup to be a Christian here', or rules that people have said you must keep in order to be a 'Proper Christian,' e.g. 'You need to speak in tongues.'

Promises & Promises

You can give a short talk illustrating the point of **verses 15-18** by using the sentence 'Will Christ give grace?' as a visual aid.

WILL:
The promise is like a will (**verse 15**). You can't change the mind of the deceased. God's not dead, but His promise is equally fixed. He won't break it.

CHRIST:
The use of the singular 'seed' rather than 'seeds' (**verse 16**) identifies that the promise to Abraham was not just to his descendants but would come to fulfilment in Christ, one man.

GIVE:
If the Judaizers (remember them) were on the ball, then the giving of land and life came through keeping the law. But you can't have it both ways. It is either promise or law. We have already seen that the promise cannot be overturned so the promise has to be the way (**verse 17**). The law must have some other part to play in God's purposes.

GRACE:
God gave us the inheritance (eternal life). He gave it (past tense), it has already happened. This is an act of grace (**verse 18**). It is unilateral; this means it is an action taken by one side without requiring corresponding action from the other side.

Second Hand News

The old game of 'Chinese Whispers' is a good illustration of **verses 19 & 20**. Pass a short message on to the person next to you in a whisper that only they can hear. Do it quickly and do not repeat the message. They then pass the message on to their neighbour and so on down the line. Compare the message received at the far end with that which was originally sent.

Passing the message directly from the start of the line to the end would have been one way to ensure it did not get misunderstood. Read **verses 19 & 20**. The law came through an intermediary — Moses. **Acts 7:53** and **Hebrews 2:2** also imply the second intermediary of God's angels. The promise came to Abraham first hand from God. The more important message came directly.

Law Abiding

Talk about some laws which get broken easily and are difficult to police. Examples might be selling cigarettes to under 16's, 30mph speed limits, litter dropping.

The thing about rules is that, however arbitrary they seem to be, if you draw a line somewhere, you can say when someone has broken the rule. 31mph is speeding; 29mph isn't.

Invite your group to invent a new rule, which everyone must obey for the rest of the meeting. An example might be, 'Everyone who speaks must cross their legs first'.

Read **verses 21 & 22**. God's law enabled His people to know when they were being disobedient. The law shows the need for the promise. It's not petty, arbitrary or stupid. It's dead clever and extremely generous.

We are not prisoners of it (**verse 23**) or managed strictly by it (**verse 24**), but led from it, to Jesus. He is our new supervisor (**verse 25**), but He is not a jailer or a strict tutor. He gives us freedom.

Equality

Think about your church. Are there barriers between sexes, races or rank.

Look at the *Work-Out* sheet. Get members, working individually, to fill in the prejudice box. Invite any who are prepared to share their answers to do so, but it is not to be made compulsory.

Huddles

Huddles is a simple game. Everyone huddles together in the middle of the room. You shout out a small number and members get into groups of that number. If you don't get in a group of the correct number you are out. Keep going until there are only two left. Explain that although this game excluded people, the Gospel is inclusive. Read **Galatians 3:28**.

➤ DOING IT

Memory Verse

Learn **Galatians 3:28**. The law identified our failure, but there is unity and hope in the Gospel.

Pray

Lead a time of prayer which includes confession and forgiveness. Pray for any prejudice we have about other members of the Body of Christ to be forgiven, and that we might have the resolve to work out fresh relationships.

MEMORY VERSE

There is neither Jew nor Greek, slave nor free, male nor female, for you are all one in Christ Jesus.

Galatians 3:28

ELEVATION

The rules we sometimes initiate in our church are:

People have said that to be a proper Christian you must:

PREJUDICE BOX

'I think in our church I fail to recognise the equality of......'

'The reason for this is........'

Behind My Back
Galatians 4:1-20

◆ **TEACHING POINT**

This session focuses on the subject of wholeheartedness.

◆ **GROUP AIM**

That members should remember what they once were and determine not to fall back into old ways.

✎ **EQUIPMENT CHECKLIST**

- ❑ Bibles
- ❑ *Work-Out* sheets
- ❑ Three shoe boxes, one wrapped as a pass-the-parcel containing a small cross
- ❑ Music for pass-the-parcel
- ❑ Flipchart or Overhead projector
- ❑ A dry-wipe board and pens
- ❑ Pencils

☞ **LEADERS' GUIDE**

There is a danger with wholeheartedness meetings. The first danger is never to do them; but all Christians tend to backslide unless pointed to the Gospel regularly. The second danger, perhaps slightly more subtle, is to do them all the time. You become the sort of group where every meeting is a challenge to fuller and deeper commitment. This becomes really draining, especially if you are a committed Christian member who really can't offer any more.

As soon as you focus attention on the church leadership there is a risk of the session drifting into criticism. Watch out for this in the last part of *Teaching It*.

☞ **BIBLE BACKGROUND**

The image of slavery is powerful. It is hard for us to understand it since it has now been abolished. Paul relates the position of a child to that of a slave. The child is subject to the rules and regulations of the household. When God's people were under law, before Jesus, they were like slaves, but they have now grown up into adults and heirs. They are free. (**verses 1-7**).

Paul doesn't do many jokes. There is a play on words in this passage that only works in Greek. The same word for 'principles' can mean both good and basic principles and the natural principles of earthy religion (paganism for instance). He uses both meanings of the word in **Galatians 4:3&9**. The New International Version translates one 'basic' and the other 'miserable'. It's a good translation, but it isn't funny.

Paul despairs that the Galatians are going back to old habits. He fears that he has wasted his time (**verses 8-11**).

It also seems as if the Galatians, happy to accept an infirm Paul into their midst, ceased to obey him once his teaching became unpopular (**verses 12-16**). Much of our reading of the Bible can be hindered if we take the Galatian approach. We obey the bits we like and ignore the unpopular stuff. But the challenge to the Bible scholar, preacher and indeed youth leader is to treat all Scripture even-handedly and to teach that which is difficult as well as the nice parts.

It all comes down to relationships, as indeed will your youthwork. Paul's relationship with the Galatians means he longs to see them and be with them to help them apply the more difficult teaching and to enjoy the fullness of the Gospel. He suspects that others are trying to influence the Galatians out of more sinister motives (**verses 17-20**).

➤ STARTING IT

You Don't Really Understand

Use the *Work-Out* sheet to get members into the idea, if they haven't grasped it already, that Galatians is Paul's response to problems he has heard about in the church. On the *Work-Out* sheet are some letters, replying to problems. Ask members, working in groups if necessary, to see if they can guess what the problems were.

Trappings

Thinking back to the previous sessions, discuss why the trappings of religion are so attractive. Why do we end up liking our favourite chorus more than God?

Bolivia

Your church has mysteriously been beamed down into the Bolivian jungle. It's the sort of thing that happens in Bible studies all the time. Which of the items on the *Work-Out* sheet do you think will be most useful? Do it individually, then work with a partner to score the items in order of importance 1-15.

Discuss which of the items are the 'trappings' of our culture.

➤ TEACHING IT

Slave For A Minute

Draw lots. The winners can choose someone else to be their slave for a minute. Prepare a set of cards with various forfeits on. The slaves must carry these out. E.g. make a cup of tea; wash my feet; do ten press-ups. You can think of others.

Read **verses 1-7**. Draw out the differences, using a flip-chart or overhead projector, between slaves and children. Explain why Paul was keen for those who, in a position to be treated as God's children opted for slavery, to change. Stress the great intimacy of the expression 'Abba' (**verse 6**), but don't equate it with 'Daddy'. Abba has greater overtones of strictness and obedience than 'Daddy' implies.

If you want a diversion, take time out to read the parable of the prodigal son in **Luke 15:11-32**. Notice how the son who came to his senses didn't expect sonship to remain his; he expected to be treated as one of his father's hired men (**Luke 11:17-21**). How quickly we all lose our excitement and expectation at being God's children.

Old Habits

Prepare for this by making a pass-the-parcel package with a small cross, in a shoebox, in the centre. Place it out of sight of the group.

Make a list of all the 'religious things' that members of the group do. Write each one on an index card. Try to include everything from 'singing choruses' to 'making the tea after church', however trivial it might seem.

Put two further shoeboxes on the floor. One for 'the actual package' and one for 'wrapping paper'. Get members to divide the cards into the essentials of faith (the actual package) and the optional extras (wrapping paper). Wrap up the 'essentials' parcel, using the same wrapping paper (newspaper will do) as you used on the concealed box. Place it on one side, out of sight, next to the prepared package. Chuck out the 'wrapping' box.

Play pass-the-parcel. Members will discover that the cross is the central essential of the Christian faith. But the Galatians were going back to the miserable old principles that sufficed before the cross (read **verses 8-11**).

Let's All Fall Out With The Minister

Brainstorm the things **verses 12-16** tell us about the Galatians. Hopefully the group will cotton on to things like:
>Did Paul no wrong (**verse 12**)
>Coped with Paul's illness (**verses 13&14**)
>Welcoming (**verse 14**)
>Lost their joy (**verse 15**)
>Didn't like the truth (**verse 16**)

Brainstorm the things **verses 17-20** tell us about Paul. These are a little harder to spot:
>Saw people's motives (**verse 17**)
>Encouraged consistent behaviour (**verse 18**)
>Really concerned about the Galatians (**verse 19**)
>Longed to visit (**verse 20**)

The Galatians didn't allow themselves to be put off Paul's teaching by his illness. In fact they really coped with him. But they did fall into the trap of falling out over theology. We should not fall into the trap of assessing our minister on the basis of his health, his good looks or how 'nice' we find his teaching. The only criteria is.........*(why not ask the members to suggest answers before you fill in the gap)*........whether he is faithful to the message of the apostles.

➤ DOING IT

Summer Eyes

Summer eyes only see sunny things. Make sure your summary is not too summery. Paul's desire to see the Galatians make a wholehearted commitment included these hard things:

- **They weren't to be Christians only when he was around;**
- **They weren't to ignore those bits of teaching that they didn't like.**

Pray, in small groups if necessary, for total commitment to the apostles' teaching (The Gospel).

Wipe Clean

If you can get hold of a dry wipe board then this exercise works particularly well, but it's not impossible without, you'll just have to be a bit clever.

Brainstorm onto the dry-wipe board things that members of the group say they have been zealous about, but which are really only wrapping paper, or worse, a red herring.

When all the ideas are written down, wipe them off roughly, using one downward stroke and one horizontal, to make the shape of a cross. Use this as a visual aid while you pray a prayer of recommitment for anyone who wants to do this.

WORK-OUT

DEAR RICK,

We all feel angry at times. I'm sure the referee was quite right to send you off for doing that. Perhaps you can undergo surgery for the injury to your nose when the scars have healed, but don't take the law into your own hands again.

DEAR RACHEL,

What do you mean, 'They take that sort of thing into account when pricing the goods.' It's thanks to people like you that the prices are so high. You mustn't do that again.

DEAR PETER,

No, I don't think that was a wise thing to do. I'm sure that, in time, the right girlfriend will come along. There is no need to act quite so impatiently again. I bet Kylie wasn't the slightest bit impressed.

DEAR SANDRA,

This is not a very wise use of your money. Perhaps you can find a hobby that doesn't involve quite so much time spent in dangerous parts of the town at night.

❖ ❖ ❖ B O L I V I A ❖ ❖ ❖

The Bible in English
Prayer book
Song book (music copy)
Song books (words copies)
Cassette player
Guitar
Communion cups
Ministers robes

The Bible in Spanish
(the main language of Bolivia)
English-Spanish dictionary
Teach yourself Spanish
Piano
Praise and worship tapes
Some candles and matches
A map of Bolivia

SESSION 7

Maid To Last
Galatians 4:21-31

◆ **TEACHING POINT**

That Christians are children of promise.

◆ **GROUP AIM**

To learn that actions, impatience and accidents of birth will not affect God's promise of eternal life for Christians.

✎ **EQUIPMENT CHECKLIST**

❑ Bibles
❑ Flip chart paper or OHP acetates
❑ Work-Out sheets
❑ A coin
❑ A Bible Dictionary (for preparation)

☞ **LEADERS' GUIDE**

For this passage you'll need a Bible Dictionary. The passage assumes you'll be familiar with Abraham, Sarah, Hagar, Ishmael, Isaac, Mount Sinai and Jerusalem. If you are familiar with these people and places we're well impressed. Wanna write the next book? If not, you'll find a Bible Dictionary handy. We have listed some names in our own 'mini dictionary' on page 59.

This is a hard passage. It is also true that much of Galatians teaches one point. This can be seen as a reason to skimp on the details and keep making the same point – don't. Help your members to understand the particular point that Paul is making here and why it was so important for his readers to grasp it.

☞ **BIBLE BACKGROUND**

If you haven't yet felt compelled to read **Genesis chapters 12-25**, the story of Abraham, the time is not far off when you will need to in order to understand Galatians.

Galatians 4:21-31 is aimed at those who *'desire to be under law'* more than they desire freedom in Christ (**4:21**).

Galatians 4:22-23 speaks to those Galatians who felt safe because of God's promise to Abraham. They were relying on family inheritance to save them. John the Baptist blew up this argument in **Matthew 3:7-10**. You can't just presume to be safe by being a child of Abraham. God can ignore you if you do not turn to Christ. Indeed God can raise ancestors out of a load of old rocks if He wants.

Paul explains this by pointing to Abraham's two sons, Ishmael and Isaac. Isaac is the son of the promise and so leads to freedom. His birth was unnatural given the age of his parents. Ishmael is the son of slavery. His birth was natural, but the result of impatience with God and trying to short cut the promise of a son to Abraham. Paul sees this as illustrative of slavery to the law compared to freedom in Christ.

Galatians 4:24-27 makes clear the way Paul is using the story of Isaac and Ishmael.

He sees Hagar as the mother of slavery to the Law, and Jerusalem as a place of slavery to the Law. Even the promise from **Isaiah 54:1**, quoted at **verse 27** was only partially fulfilled with the return of the nation of Israel from captivity in Babylon to Jerusalem. But Sarah, Isaac's mother, is the mother of freedom and the existence of the Christian church is the complete fulfilment of **Isaiah 54:1**.

Galatians 4:28-31 reminds those who think they have taken the easier course, to follow the spiritual line from Isaac, that they must expect persecution, although they will receive the inheritance.

➤ STARTING IT

Silly Rules

★ ★ ★

There is a number of games on this theme. The idea is to guess the rule and then keep it. The games are best played sitting in a circle with two or three people who know the rule and the rest ignorant.

The scissors game is an example. You pass a pair of closed scissors round the group saying either, 'I pass these scissors to you crossed' or, 'I pass these scissors to you uncrossed'. The secret of getting it right is nothing to do with the scissors. You either have your legs crossed or uncrossed as you make the statement and your statement must match the state of your legs. After each statement, the person leading this activity says 'Yes' if the statement is correct, and 'No' if it is wrong.

If you have members with less than two legs this is an unsatisfactory ice-breaker. It will also be a test of how many can remember that you did a similar exercise when you invented new rules for Session 5. If they remember, recap the main point of session 5, 'the joy of freedom in Christ'.

A second game on the same theme is called 'I'm going to America'. Members of the group take it in turns to say what they are taking to America with them. The rule is that the item must begin with the same letter as their Christian name. So I might say, 'I'm going to America, and I'm taking some sausages.' This would be O.K. because my name is Steve. However I couldn't take bacon, eggs or toast. Get it?

Keep playing until everyone has got it, or the last few are begging to be put out of their misery. Decide if you want to tell them, or just stop and leave them guessing.

At the end, explain that this session will be talking about more problems Paul had with the group who wanted to say that there were special rules, traditions and ceremonies you had to keep to be a Christian.

➤ TEACHING IT

Chips And Old Blocks

Ask members to explain what physical characteristics they have inherited from their parents. Use the *Work-Out* sheet question to start with. You could illustrate this on flip-chart paper or acetate as you go on. Or ask a talented member to draw cartoons of father and son, mother and daughter etc.

Go on to ask what temperamental characteristics have been inherited. Members may share they find it difficult to be punctual because their Dad is always late, or they are good at maths because their Mum is an accountant. Make a list on acetate or flip-chart paper.

Read **Galatians 4:21-31**. It is a difficult passage so it is best read by a leader.

Just because Jews counted Abraham as their physical ancestor, it doesn't mean that they will inherit the promises he received. It is a spiritual inheritance, to do with God's grace not family fortune. Explain this.

Complex Persecution

Rehearse the ways Paul and Jesus were persecuted. This is always a sobering balance to the idea that the freedom of the Gospel somehow leads to a cushy life. Re-read **verse 29** where Paul explains how this was true for Isaac and his ancestors.

Chucking Out Time

Ask the group to look at **Genesis 21:10**. (Read **verses 8-10** if they are not familiar with the context.) Give out the cards from the *Work-Out* sheet Name cards. Ask members to note down their reactions as if they were that person. Use the response at the bottom of the *Work-out* sheet or to avoid written responses, use a small portable tape-recorder and record the responses one after the other, then play the whole tape.

The fact is that a verse which Jews had traditionally interpreted as a sure sign that God excluded Gentiles from God's inheritance, Paul re-interprets as a verse that excludes non-Christian Jews.

Impatience

Get members to finish the sentence, 'The most impatient thing I have ever done is.........'

Teach them, from **Genesis chapter 16** that Abraham, although given a promise that he would have descendants at a ripe old age, did not have the patience to hang on to the promise and tried to short-cut the promise by making love to his wife's maidservant. Paul sees this as a picture of the way God deals with His people, not through the maidservant – that way only becomes an illustration of drudgery, but through the free maid (Sarah) – an illustration of freedom.

It's a really hard passage and people have struggled with it over the years. But being a Christian is a privilege and we must not get impatient about wanting the good things God has promised us. It is about being, as well as doing.

Abraham needed to relax in the promises but was impatient. We need to enjoy the blessings of God's grace and freedom. This means our perspective on life must be long-term. Members may think it is a long time until they die aged 75 or whatever, but our future perspective must go beyond the grave if the Christian life is to mean anything at all.

➤ DOING IT

Pray

Why not pray for scholars and others who work to translate and explain the Scriptures. Passages like this one show how hard this job is.

In a time of open prayer ask for volunteers to pray aloud. then toss a coin and they only get to pray if it's 'tails'. Sometimes God's plans seem completely arbitrary, but He is at work in a particular and special way. From our perspective it can be hard to fathom, but God is in control.

WORK-OUT

Family fortunes

I'm like my Mum because...

I'm like my Dad because...

NAME CARDS

My Name Is:
Hagar

My Name Is:
Sarah

My Name Is:
Ishmael

My Name Is:
Isaac

My Name Is:
Abraham

My Name Is:
A Jew today

My Name Is:
Paul

RESPONSE

My response is:

Crunch Time
Galatians 5:1-12

◆ TEACHING POINT
We must be aware of things that threaten our faith,
and keep that faith active.

◆ GROUP AIM
To alert members to dangers and opportunities regarding
their faith.

✎ **EQUIPMENT CHECKLIST**
- ❑ Bibles
- ❑ Glass vessel, water, ink
- ❑ Clothes, knife, fork, plate, die, chocolate
- ❑ *Work-Out* sheets
- ❑ 4 pieces of card
- ❑ Tennis balls, skittles/lemonade bottles, a way of marking out a goal
- ❑ OHP & acetates/large sheet of paper

☞ **LEADERS' GUIDE**
The passages we look at in this session and the next have a lot to say about the theme of freedom. Keep an eye on the news for examples of people gaining or losing freedom and bring these examples in as illustrations for the session. This would be a good session in which to use one of the 'freedom' icebreakers at the front of this book.

☞ **BIBLE BACKGROUND**
What is it that counts? That's the crunch question in this passage. Paul knows that there's a great struggle going on within the Galatians as they swing back and forth between the way of freedom and a return to slavery. No doubt the Judaizers were feeding the Galatians plenty of plausible arguments for why their way was right: but Paul weighs in with the astonishing and wonderful key to the whole issue in **verse 6**. *'The only thing that counts is faith expressing itself through love'.* You may like to ponder the relationship of this statement with that in **6:15** – *'what counts is a new creation'* – faith again is the key.

➤ STARTING IT

Messing It Up
✪ ✪
Show the group a big glass of clean water (or a jug or bowl with sides you can see through) and drop a little ink into it. Use just enough so that all the water is noticeably coloured (practise beforehand to find how much you need!).

Introduce the session with the principle, which you have just demonstrated, that is stated in **verse 9**: some things can be utterly changed by adding a little of some other substance. That idea lies behind the whole of this session.

Paul is presenting the Galatians with a crucial challenge as to which way they are going, and it will take only a step in the wrong direction to send them completely wrong.

Chocodash

Listen to the passage together and ask the group to suggest the main idea that comes out of it, before moving on to the next activity.

You'll need a die, a set of clothes (for example a coat, hat, scarf, gloves and plastic over-trousers), a plate, knife and fork and a **BIG!!** bar of chocolate. Everyone sits around in a circle and throws the die in turn. When someone throws a six he/she runs to the middle of the circle, puts on the clothes and then tries to eat as much of the chocolate as possible, cutting each individual square off with the knife and fork. In the meantime the rest of the group continue throwing the die. Whenever someone throws a six they run to the middle and take over the clothes, cutlery and chocolate. No one is allowed to start eating the chocolate until they have the clothes on. This usually develops into a fast, furious and very funny game. Continue until either the group or the chocolate is exhausted.

Draw out of the wreckage the fact that one of the strongest feelings that comes out of this game is frustration. We wait ages for a six to come up and then suddenly we are released, set for the glorious freedom of stuffing ourselves on chocolate. And then someone else (doubtless by a mixture of low cunning and outright cheating) throws a six and we are torn away from the chocolate and stuck back in the circle, with only the outside chance of another six to give us hope.

Input

The last activity may seem a trivial example, but essentially it is what Paul is challenging the Galatians about in **verse 1**: they are actually in danger of **choosing** to go back into the circle, having tasted the rewards of freedom. What a stupid thing to do! He tells them, 'Don't do it!' and in **verses 2-4** he explains why. Make sure the group understand this before you move on.

➤ TEACHING IT

Reward!

Give each group member a copy of the *Work-Out* sheet and ask them to work in pairs to come up with the most appropriate reward for each activity mentioned on it. They need not all be entirely serious. Take some time to hear people's ideas.

Point out that 'Telling someone the best news they could possibly hear' is precisely what Paul was doing by telling the Gospel, yet his 'reward' for it was persecution (**verse 11**). Paul identifies the reason for his persecution as *'the offence of the cross'*. Ask the group for ideas as to why people may find the message of the cross offensive — what Paul had mainly in mind was pride, which makes us resent the idea that we can't save ourselves, but welcome other reasons that the group may have identified in people they know. Paul was very clear about which side of the freedom/slavery divide he is on, and he stuck to it despite the trouble it brought. This leads on to the next activity.

Roller Blocker

Mark out a goal at one end of the room and mark a point a few yards away for the roller to stand on. Give the roller several tennis balls. All he or she has to do is roll the balls along the floor into the goal. However, you also nominate a blocker, who is allowed to position a number of skittles (lemonade-type bottles will do, but beware the fizz later on if you use full ones!) about midway between the roller and the goal. Have enough skittles ready to make the game a challenge for even accomplished rollers, but make sure that the roller always has at least a theoretical chance. The blocker can move the skittles around, but not while the ball is in transit.

Give as many people as possible a go at both roles. If this game doesn't lead to frustration for the roller, you're skimping on the skittles!

Input

Now look with the group at **verse 7**. The Galatians had been clear about where they were going but someone had blocked their way, keeping them from the truth. Even worse, they were accepting that situation. (If you had rollers in the group who gave up in despair during *'Roller Blocker'*, you might point out the similarity here.)

Under Attack

If your group members already know the 'Parable of the Sower' (**Matthew 13:3-9**), check that they know what the different bits of it mean (**Matthew 13:19-23**). If not, tell the parable and briefly explain it.

Now put 4 cards up on the wall at different points. They should read *'I don't understand God'*, *'Having a hard time because of Jesus'*, *'Having a good time without Jesus'* and *'Life's just too tough'*. If you can add appropriate visual images to the cards, either drawn or cut out of magazines, so much the better in terms of impact.

Explain that these cards cover the problems which Jesus mentions in His explanation of the parable (the seed among thorns gets two cards because it covers two forms of worldly problem). Ask the group to think in silence about the week that's just gone. Have there been things under any or all of these four headings which have threatened their reliance on Jesus, or have stopped them trusting Him altogether?

Allow a couple of minutes for them to think, while you play some quiet music. Then read **verse 7** again aloud, and pray aloud for those who have spotted a source of trouble, particular if it's one that's likely to crop up again. Remind people that the parable ends on a note of joy and hope, and read **verse 5** a couple of times: it's possible for us to continue *'running a good race'* if we keep our gaze fixed on Jesus.

It's important that you give people an opportunity to follow this exercise up with a leader after the session if they want to do so.

➤ DOING IT

Free Expression

Verse 6 raises two big issues for our members (and all of us) — are we trusting in Jesus and are we expressing that in loving ways? The first of these issues will have been addressed more than once as you've worked through this resource.

Get the group to brainstorm a list of people they may meet tomorrow. Get at least a couple of ideas from each member. Write names/descriptions on an OHP or a large sheet of paper. Now ask the question: 'How can I express my faith in love to these people?' Encourage members to think of ways which are as practical as possible. Have a couple of minutes to pray through the ideas, silently or aloud. Encourage people to pray a prayer pledging that they will try to show love in these ways and asking God to help them.

Summary

Summarise briefly this session, and look together at **Galatians 5:6** as a memory verse — for learning either now or individually during the week. Stress that this is a verse which should spur us into action.

MEMORY VERSE

For in Christ Jesus neither circumcision nor uncircumcision has any value. The only thing that counts is faith expressing itself through love.

Galatians 5:6

What rewards do you think should be given for these heroic acts?

REWARDS

✦ Walking the dog every day for a month for the lady next door, who is ill.

✦ Giving your mum flowers when it's her birthday.

✦ Telling someone the best news they could possibly hear.

✦ Single-handedly rescuing the national music industry with your debut CD.

✦ Babysitting for Dennis the Menace.

✦ Giving your mum flowers when it's not her birthday.

✦ Calling an ambulance when someone collapses in the street.

✦ Saving a roomful of tiny children from a horrible death at the hands of the evil Zarg from the planet Vogon.

Failure and Fruit
Galatians 5:13-25

◆ **TEACHING POINT**

To teach that all the Fruit of the Spirit are equally important.

◆ **GROUP AIM**

To encourage group members behaviour to reflect *all* the Fruit of the Spirit as part of their normal Christian life.

✎ **EQUIPMENT CHECKLIST**

❑ Bibles
❑ Rope
❑ Fruit

❑ Magazines and newspapers
❑ *Work-Out* sheets

☞ **LEADERS' GUIDE**

It will probably come as no surprise that in this session we spend quite a bit of time thinking about the Fruit of the Spirit. Don't let familiarity breed contempt, even if you have members in your group who were introduced to this passage in the cradle.

One of the most important messages to get across when thinking about the fruit is that it is not something that is added as an extra layer on top of our 'normal' way of living: our old way of life needs to be replaced by the characteristics which are brought forth by the Spirit.

This is a real struggle for all of us from time to time, if not constantly, and we owe it to our group members to prepare them for it and to help them in the struggle. So, we've tried to keep the session practical and as light as possible, but if all that comes out of it is a warm, fuzzy glow based on 'love, joy and peace' then something's gone wrong.

☞ **BIBLE BACKGROUND**

This passage, like the one we looked at last time, starts with a reminder that we're called to be free. However, while continuing the theme that we are saved by faith in Jesus it also answers the inevitable question, 'If we are relying for our salvation only on what Jesus has done for us, do we need to bother about the way we live?' The answer is that we do, because the way we live is a sure sign of whether we are being led along by God's Spirit or by our sinful nature. These are always at war in our lives, but we must give primacy to the Spirit (**verses 17, 24-25**).

Paul points us in **verse 14** to a single command to guide our relations with other people. He would have known full well that there is a still greater command which governs our relations with God (**Mark 12:29-31**). Here, though, he is concentrating on how the Galatians should treat each other, and **verse 15** suggests that this message was urgently needed.

In pointing to how Christians should live Paul was not re-introducing the Law by the back door. He saw that following the Law is massively different from living a life which honours Christ and reinforces the Gospel message. See **1 Corinthians 9:20-21**, where Paul can say with no hint of confusion, '...*I myself am not under the law...though I am not free from God's law but am under Christ's law.*' He also speaks in other places of 'obedience' as a necessary result of faith (eg **Romans 1:5**, **2 Thessalonians 1:8**).

Note in this context that the Fruit of the Spirit is not the Gospel. In itself the fruit is worthless, in that displaying it can never put us right with God. Its value comes in the context of a life lived in trust in Jesus. Then it brings honour to Him and shows, through our transformed lives, that we are controlled by His Spirit and not by our old self.

➤ STARTING IT

Thinking Back

Read or listen to **verses 13 & 14**. See who can remember last week's memory verse, and discuss briefly about how it is expanded here.

Tug-Of-War

If you have space, rope and a suitable group have a straight tug-of-war. If conditions are muddy, so much the better but bear in mind the laundry bill...

A good substitute tug-of-war can be achieved by having each team link arms and pull sideways: the front person of each team links arms with the front person of the other team.

This is good fun but be aware of the potential for pile-ups and don't put small people between gorillas unless you have a surgeon on site. If a team has to break its link then the people still linked to the other team can keep pulling, but the rest have to sit it out.

Read or listen to the whole passage together and ask which verse or verses seem to bear most relation to the tug-of-war activity. If **verse 17** does not feature in the answers, try reading the passage again but stopping after, say, **verse 17**. Ask if this conflict is something people have experienced in their own attempts to follow Jesus and 'express their faith through love'; if so, encourage them to share a little bit about it but don't push them further than they're comfortable with.

Fruitfest

Present the group with a range of different fruits, preferably including some unusual ones: most big supermarkets have a fair selection. Allow everybody to choose and eat one item, then ask why they made those choices. Some fruits will emerge as more popular than others.

Read **verses 22 & 23** and point out that the qualities of which Paul speaks are not individual fruits; together they make up the Fruit of the Spirit. We can't pick and choose which qualities we like the sound of and ignore the others (such as, for most of us, self-control). If we're taking Jesus seriously we should be looking for all of them.

➤ TEACHING IT

Fruit In Action

Ask the group to work in pairs. Each pair should take one or two of the bits of fruit listed in **verses 22 & 23** and come up with examples of how they might appear in everyday life. This may be done by acting a quick sketch or by devising some kind of case study. Encourage the pairs to use situations which might occur in their own lives. The sketches or case studies should be shared with the rest of the group.

Getting The Balance

Give the group a pile of magazines and newspapers. Have them make one set of cuttings (adverts, 'news' stories etc) illustrating the kind of things Paul speaks of in **verses 19-21**, and another set illustrating the fruit he speaks of in **verses 22 & 23**. The chances are pretty high that the second set of cuttings will be much smaller (unless all your magazines are of the 'St Francis of Assisi Monthly' variety). However, this is the lifestyle we are called to as Christians.

Ask the group how they feel about this. It may seem daunting to know that we're going to be in the minority in valuing and striving to develop the Fruit of the Spirit. Encourage the group to look through the passage and find one reason to stick to this lifestyle at all costs. They'll probably come up with the second half of **verse 21**. Quite right too. We need to keep coming back to the eternal dimension in order to help motivate us for grinding on from day to day when things are tough. Paul did this – see **verse 5** of this chapter. The rest of our motivation comes from gratitude for what Jesus has done for us; another big Galatians theme.

It may help your group if you point out that the end of **verse 21** is talking about people for whom sexual immorality and all the rest, are a regular and accepted part of life, not those who slip up from time to time but are concerned to be led by the Spirit.

Bonus Time!

Ask for a volunteer from the group and set them a task which it is impossible for them to do alone – like reaching something which you have fixed too

high up for them – but which would be easily achieved with a partner.
If they don't think of asking for help, give it long enough to get them really
frustrated and then ask someone else to help them. Let them share their
feelings about what has happened.

Not Alone

What we've seen so far about living as God wants may make people feel like
the volunteer; they've been set a task which is beyond them. Look together at
verse 24. By turning to Christ a fundamental change happens to us. Our sinful
nature is crucified – that is, its power is broken. That is something that God does
for us. He is in the position of the second person, who helped the volunteer
achieve the task.

Assure people that if we are God's then He will surely help us. We work with
Him, not on our own, to keep in step with the Spirit (**verse 25**).

➤ DOING IT

On The Case

Distribute copies of the *Work-Out* sheet and ask people to work in pairs and
come up with answers to the situations included on it.

Summary

Summarise briefly this session, and look together at **Galatians 5:25** as a
memory verse – for learning either now or individually during the week. It's a
short and sweet reminder of the need to work with God to produce a life
which pleases Him.

Pray

Have a time for prayer, either aloud or in silence. Suggest that people write
on the bottom of the *Work-Out* sheet the names of those qualities within the
Fruit of the Spirit that they particularly feel need developing in their lives. Then
they should pray for these things. Have a time of thanksgiving based around
verse 24.

MEMORY VERSE

*Since we live by the Spirit, let us
keep in step with the Spirit.*

Galatians 5:25

WORK-OUT

1. You have been trying to do a job by yourself instead of asking for help. Because of this it has gone wrong and you have caused some damage.

⇨ **What Fruit of the Spirit should now dominate your thinking and behaviour?**

⇨ **How are you going to go about putting things right?**

⇨ **Is it the absence of a particular fruit that has caused this problem in the first place?**

2. You are walking home from school. Two boys from the year above you walk menacingly towards you. You are alone in the street. As they reach you, one picks up a piece of wood from the pavement. The other asks you if you have any money. You have no money.

⇨ **Which Fruit of the Spirit is going to be of most use to you in the next two minutes?**

3. Your parents have imposed a curfew on you because you have exams approaching. This weekend there are two parties and a youth group sleepover which you really want to go to. Attending any one of these would involve breaking the curfew.

⇨ **Which Fruit of the Spirit is going to be of most use to you in coping with this situation?**

4. You are on your way to a friend's house three miles away. You couldn't persuade anyone to give you a lift and you have no money for the bus, so you're walking. It starts to rain. You discover that you have a hole in your shoe. A passing car splashes you and the driver laughs.

⇨ **Which Fruit of the Spirit is going to be of most use to you in this situation?**

Loaded Up Or
Loaded Down
Galatians 5:26-6:18

◆ TEACHING POINT
There are two points to this session:
1. To teach that sowing by the Spirit is essential for Christian living.
2. To recap the whole of Galatians.

◆ GROUP AIM
To grasp the overall message of Galatians and to desire to live
a consistent, faithful, Christian life.

✎ **EQUIPMENT CHECKLIST**

- ❑ Bibles
- ❑ *Work-Out* sheets
- ❑ Marker pens
- ❑ Seeds

- ❑ Bulky prizes and cabbages
- ❑ OHP or flip-chart
- ❑ Pencils and paper

☞ **LEADERS' GUIDE**

There are two parts to this session. You can do it as two sessions if you want, but it's not necessary.

In the first part Paul talks about relationships and service. Have you ever met people who seemed to have the idea that they were too important to do the washing up? Not everyone grasps the principle that the Christian life is about service, not superiority. One of the mottoes of the British judicial system is, *'Be ye ever so high, the law is above ye.'* Well one of the mottoes of Christianity ought to be, *'Be ye ever so high ye can still do the dishes.'* All Christians, and especially leaders, ought to do the dishes, or take out the rubbish, or clean the drains or the toilets or something that reminds them, day by day, that it is a joy and a privilege to serve. All Christian young people ought to be introduced, at the earliest possible stage, to the principle of service, and given the opportunity to serve.

In the second part (**verses 11-18**) Paul concludes the whole letter with a summary of his thinking. He recaps some of the 'Sacred Cows' that the Judaizers were sticking with, pointing, once again to the centrality of the Gospel and, in particular, the Cross of Christ.

☞ **BIBLE BACKGROUND**

5:26: This verse is better understood as an introduction to **chapter six** than a conclusion to **chapter five**. Conceit, provocation and envy are all problems with getting your relationships out of balance.

6:2-5: We can take this as a rebuke if we are not bearing the burdens of others. But we ought to be equally rebuked if we are not allowing others to share our burdens. It is a sign of weakness to think you can cope by yourself.

There is no contradiction between **verses 2 & 5**. We should share burdens, but our load (a different Greek word) is our personal responsibility to God. Nobody can bear this for us.

6:6-10: The metaphor that holds this section together is sowing and reaping. Whatever you sow, so shall you reap. This is then applied not just to doing good, but also to appropriate thinking and teaching.

6:11-18: This is more than just a summary. Paul grabs the pen off his scribe and writes himself in *'large letters'* (**verse 11**). In summarising he manages a discourse on the nature of Christianity, a three point sermon on the nature of the church, a personal request for support and, having spent six chapters correcting and rebuking, he ends with The Grace.

A letter from Paul dropping through the post-box was probably a sure sign that something in the early church needed to change.

➤ STARTING IT

Cabbages

Many years ago, the television programme Crackerjack had a quiz game in which a correct answer to a question gained the contestant a prize, an incorrect answer a cabbage, and contestants had to hold all their prizes and cabbages during the quiz. Dropping anything gained them an extra cabbage and they were eliminated at three cabbages.

Use this as a warm-up activity with cheap, bulky prizes and loads of cabbages (maybe your local greengrocers will sell you some old ones that pong a bit).

Point out **verse 2** that teaches us to bear one another's burdens and not try to cope in our own strength.

➤ TEACHING IT

Self-Opinion

Give out copies of the *Work-Out* sheet and ask people to do a brief self-assessment under the headings, 'Brains, Looks, Future and Personality'.

Having done the survey, read the group **verses 3-5**. Make no comment but allow the words to sink in before proceeding.

Sharing

Get members to share 'the best Christian truth they have ever been told' with their neighbour in the room. Then write all these truths on paper and stick them to a wall. Read **verse 6** to explain why you did this exercise.

Sow What?

Purchase some packs of seed. If you can't get 'variety' packs then buy several different types and mix them up. Then get each member to sow a seed and over the coming weeks refer back to the seeds as a visual aid of **verses 7-10**. The point to make at this time is that the eventual plant will depend on the variety of seed sown. Likewise the harvest of our lives depends on what we sow. **Galatians 5** taught us to walk by the Spirit. **Galatians 6** teaches us to sow by the Spirit.

Do Gooders

To teach **verses 1-10** as a whole, perhaps in a situation where you have little time for an in-depth study, try the following questions:

1. When was the last time you done good?
2. What did you done?
3. Who did you done it to?
4. Would you done do it again?

Share answers.

You could tell a few illustrative stories, the more up-to-date the better, of those who have suffered for doing good. At the time of writing there is a current story of a man who was kicked to death because he tried to dissuade some vandals from damaging a car.

Help members to understand that the benefit of good deeds may not be in this life, but 'at the proper time' (**verse 9**)

Dictation

As a break you could do one of the many 'dictation' games, where a boss dictates a message to a secretary on the other side of the room. The more bosses there are doing it at the same time, the harder it is to hear the message.

The brief point is the message of **verse 11** that Paul, who has been dictating his letter to a scribe/secretary up to this point, now writes in his own hand.

Sacred Cows

Put on the OHP or flip-chart the definition and picture of a Sacred Cow from the *Work-Out* sheet. Ask members of the group to think of any Sacred Cows that are obvious to them.

Remind the group that Paul had been anxious to teach the Galatians that Judaism was like a sacred cow. It was not necessary to become a Jew in order to become a Christian.

Ask the group to summarise the constants that Paul referred back to, time and time again. Hopefully they will come back to:
- Relationships   • Gospel   • Prayer

Sacred Cows undermine relationships when they're about self-preservation (**verse 12**).

Sacred Cows undermine the Gospel when they're about self-improvement (**verses 13,14**).
Sacred Cows undermine prayer when they're about self-sufficiency (**verses 16,18**).

This would make an interesting, three point talk, if your group can cope with listening to a talk for five to seven minutes.

➤ DOING IT

Memory Verse

Galatians 6:14 is an excellent memory verse of not only the whole session, but the whole of Galatians.

Summary

Galatians has raised three main questions, but before offering your group these three points as a summary, ask them what they have remembered and enjoyed.

Different people respond to summaries in different ways. Try the alternative feedback sheet in *Work-Out*. It may help. Remember that feedback, examinations and tests are all tests of your teaching, not their learning. Don't feel bad about that, but don't pressurise the young people to give 'correct' feedback. You genuinely want to know what they have picked up from these sessions in order for you to make best use of future teaching opportunities.

- Galatians has dealt with authority. Christian authority is apostolic.
- Galatians has dealt with salvation. Christian salvation is centred on the cross.
- Galatians has dealt with holiness. Christian holiness is Holy Spirit inspired.
- Christianity is apostolic, cross centred and, if you'll forgive the expression, fruity.

John Stott's summary, in the Bible Speaks Today commentary on Galatians says, 'So we have Christ through his Apostles to teach us, Christ through his cross to save us and Christ through his Spirit to sanctify us. This in a nutshell is the message of Galatians and indeed of Christianity itself.'

MEMORY VERSE

May I never boast except in the cross of our Lord Jesus Christ, through which the world has been crucified to me, and I to the world.

Galatians 6:14

Self-Opinion

Brains:	Brainbox	Bright spark	Borderline	What's a brain?
Looks:	God's gift to humankind	Nothing soap & shampoo couldn't improve	God's cruel joke	
Future:	High-powered job	Medium powered job	Lifetime of service	What job?
Person-ality:	Life and soul of the party	Occasional flashes of wit	Dullard	Get a life first

SACRED COW
A sacred Cow is an idea or institution, unreasonably held to be above criticism.

Alternative Feedback Sheet

If Galatians was a meal it would be:

If Galatians was an animal it would be:

If Galatians was a car it would be:

If Galatians was a building it would be:

Galatians Dictionary

Who Are They?

Paul The persecutor formerly known as Saul. The boss man, letter writer and church planter.

Jesus Christ The Saviour of the world, came from God, born a man, lived (taught), died and rose again.

Peter The Rock (once called Simon), Apostle and evangelist.

James The Lord's brother, leader of the Jewish Christian Church at Jerusalem. Martyred by stoning in AD61, according to the historian, Josephus.

Barnabas Paul's companion and constant encouragement, always spoken of warmly.

Titus A Greek, and one of Paul's most trusted companions, often used to deliver correspondence or sort out difficult situations.

John Apostle and another pillar of the Jerusalem church.

Abraham Patriarch and spiritual ancestor. Called by God in Genesis 12 to leave his home and trust God for land and descendants, even in his old age.

Hagar Egyptian bond-servant to Abraham's household, servant to Abraham's wife, Sarah. Encouraged by Sarah to have sex with Abraham and conceive a child at a time when Sarah and Abraham were both impatient and doubting God's promise. The son conceived was Ishmael.

Isaac Abraham's son by Sarah. His name means 'laughing joy' because he was born to Sarah when she was very old and it was believed to be a miracle. Considered to be the 'son of freedom'.

Ishmael Abraham's son by Hagar, Sarah's handmaid. He was the result of Abraham and Sarah's impatience and lack of faith in God's promise of a son. Considered to be the 'son of slavery'.

Sarah Abraham's wife and mother of Isaac. Her lack of faith in God's promise of a son lead her to give her handmaid, Hagar, to Abraham to have sex with and bear him a son, Ishmael.

Where Is It?

Galatia Ephesus, Corinth, Philippi, Thessalonica and Colossae were all towns/cities that received letter from Paul. But Galatia? Not a city, but a region, a Roman Province. A region that, with Derbe, Lystra and Antioch, mentioned in Acts 13 & 14 and again in Acts 16, Paul passed through. Part of modern day Turkey.

Getting Around 'BIG'
TEACHING A WHOLE BIBLE BOOK TO YOUR GROUP

What a daunting thought, eh? A **whole** book, from the Bible, which is itself so big. How will our young people face up to it? How will **we** manage?

Well, there's no real need to be worried. Obviously, with Galatians you have this resource here to help you. And there are some basic principles which apply to other Bible books you may decide you want to teach in the future.

As with any other subject that we want to teach, there are a few essential questions that we need to think through. After that, things become a lot clearer. So, take a deep breath, and away we go...

1 Why Is The Book in The Bible? This really is a bit crucial. We need to see the book in the light of the rest of Scripture and understand how it relates to the whole revelation of God's love and work. Maybe that's pretty clear for the books of the New Testament, but we must learn to pass the Old Testament writings through a New Testament filter, to see how they relate to God's plan of salvation in Jesus.

2 What's The Main Message Of The Book? Does the author tell us why he bothered writing it? Some, like Solomon and John, tell us straight (see **Proverbs 1:1-7** and **John 20:31**); others give us hints. Look for key verses and crucial incidents that indicate major themes.

By this stage we have a handle on the book. This kind of big picture stops us from getting intimidated by the thought of dealing with a whole block of the Bible.

3. What Can We Learn From The Book About How We Should Live As Children Of God? This is the same question as we will (presumably) ask about any section of God's Word, but it needs keeping at the front of our minds, as we can easily lose sight of it when we're dealing with a large chunk of the Bible. Most books, of course, will contain many different lessons of this sort; but often there will be one or two overriding principles. Micah, for instance, hinges on **chapter 6 verse 8**; Hebrews on the worth of persevering.

All these questions together focus on the fact that we need to know the book well ourselves. Again, this should be true for any part of God's word, but when we're handling only a small part of it we can sometimes get away with not putting a lot of work into our own understanding of it. To handle a whole book confidently, and so to help our members gain from it, requires effort and time from us.

Given a solid foundation along these lines, then, what next? In practical terms, how shall we approach Bible books? Here are some crucial tips.

• Remember how to eat an elephant: one spoonful at a time. It wouldn't make a lot of sense to do the whole of Isaiah in one session except at the very shallowest level. (Shallow levels are fine, of course, as long as that's all you're trying to achieve.) Take manageable chunks.

• Don't feel you have to cover the whole book in successive sessions. Do a few weeks and then take a break. Summarise before you leave it for a while, and recap when you come back to it. It is, in any case, worth recapping as you go along — like revising for exams or watering seeds, little and often is most effective.

• If you're doing a book with a recognisable author, introduce it with a session on the author. The human interest angle helps promote interest. We don't know for certain that Isaiah was sawn in half, but the possibility gains him a bit more sympathy.

• With longer books, don't feel you must study every chapter. Focus on key incidents or follow one character or family as the book unfolds. This is part of being realistic about our teaching; there's a danger in being under-ambitious, but we shouldn't expect to be able to convey every shade of meaning in the book. If we can whet appetites for further study, that's a great result.

At the end of the day, our young people should be able to answer these questions about the book:

- What is its main thrust?
- What would we lose if it wasn't in the Bible?
- How does it relate to the good news about Jesus?
- What should we do or be like as a result of reading this book?

GO FOR IT!

Useful Resources For Understanding Whole Books

According to Plan, Graeme Goldsworthy, IVP/Lancer
How the whole Bible hangs together in terms of God's overall plan of salvation. Useful timecharts and graphics.
The Bible from Scratch, Simon Jenkins, Lion
A quick and funny introduction to Bible books and key characters. Great for giving to group members, too.
New Bible Commentary, IVP (or other one-volume Bible commentary)
Helpful, brief overviews of whole books, as well as commentary on the text.
Starting with the Old Testament and **_Starting with the New Testament_**, Stephen Travis, Lion
Short, informative, colourful guides giving an overview of background and teaching. Great introductory material.

SUPPORTING CHILDREN AND YOUTH

· **COVENANTERS** is an evangelical organisation, 'Resourcing The Local Church' in its work with children and young people by helping them to attract and hold, lead to faith in Christ and equip for service as full members of the church.

· **COVENANTERS** helps churches by offering an age structure covering 0-20 years, providing training, support and resources for leaders, and events and evangelism opportunities for group members.

· The **COVENANTER** package is Bible-based, church-controlled, inter-denominational, non-uniformed and flexible.

COVENANTERS
11/13, Lower Hillgate, STOCKPORT, Cheshire SK1 1JQ
Tel. (0161) 474 1262

Other Resources

Books that should be indispensable in a youth leader's library are:

Young People and the Bible Phil Moon (Marshalls) 1993
Christian Youth Work   Phil Moon and Mark Ashton (Monarch) 1995

Other books that CPAS/Covenanters produce which will help you teach the Bible to teenagers:

All Together Forever	Ephesians
Harping On	Six Psalms
Powered Up	Key moments from Acts
Repeat Prescription	The Ten Commandments
People with a Purpose	Ten Old Testament characters
Mission In Action	Helping your group to broaden their horizons
Pressure Points	Issues that teenagers think about
Just About Coping	Issues that teenagers have to cope with
You'd Better Believe It	Christian Doctrine
Outlawed by Grace	Galatians

And these books will help resource your meetings:

Know Ideas	Ideas to put into your programme
Know Ideas 2	More of the above
Rave On	Ideas and principles of worship
DIY Worship	A bumper package of worship resources

Other books from Covenanters

Focus on Relationships
Focus on Practical Discipleship
These two resources encourage individual teenagers to respond to questions and situations relevant to each theme. They are ideal for discussion groups. A student workbook and a leaders' guide are available for each.

What's the Score?
A short book for use in evangelism, particularly useful for those interested in football.

FROM COVENANTERS, ORDER FROM ADDRESS BELOW

CHURCH PASTORAL AID SOCIETY
Athena Drive, Tachbrook Park, WARWICK. CV34 6NG
Tel: (01926) 334242   24-hour Sales Orderline: (01926) 335855

COVENANTERS
11/13, Lower Hillgate, STOCKPORT, Cheshire SK1 1JQ
Tel: (0161) 474 1262